The World of Nature

CROCODILES AND ALLIGATORS

GALLERY BOOKS
An Imprint of W. H. Smith Publishers Inc.
112 Madison Avenue
New York City 10016

This edition first published in U.S.
in 1991 by Gallery Books,
an imprint of W.H. Smith Publishers, Inc.
112 Madison Avenue, New York, New York 10016·

ISBN 0-8317-9572-7

Printed and bound in Spain

For rights information about the photographs in
this book please contact:

The Image Bank
111 Fifth Avenue, New York, NY 10003

Producer: Solomon M. Skolnick
Writer: Scott Weidensaul
Design Concept: Lesley Ehlers
Designer: Ann-Louise Lipman
Editor: Sara Colacurto
Production: Valerie Zars
Photo Researcher: Edward Douglas
Assistant Photo Researcher: Robert V. Hale
Editorial Assistant: Carol Raguso

Title page: In a scene reminiscent of
prehistoric times, a mud-caked American
alligator, *Alligator mississippiensis,* basks
in the warm sun. *Opposite:* Several
American alligators linger near the water
in the Florida Everglades. In the days of
heavy poaching, even parks provided little
refuge to alligators.

Loglike – the perfect description of an alligator floating at the water's surface, only the top of its head and rows of armored back scales showing above the mat of green duckweed. It may sit this way for hours: motionless, eyes narrowed to slits, seemingly incapable of any but the slowest of movements.

And so in a water-logged cypress forest in Florida, a six-footer is lazing away a warm spring afternoon. The gator has done nothing but blink for nearly an hour, and seems more a feature of the landscape than a living thing.

Nearby, a purple gallinule tiptoes through the fireflag plants. The alligator slowly begins to move – not toward the bird, but toward the more open water of the swamp. The motion is smooth and somehow unreal; the gator's tail undulates quietly just beneath the surface, swirling the dark water in eddies as it propels the animal forward. Across the swamp, about 50 feet away, a second, somewhat smaller alligator is sunning itself, apparently intruding on the larger reptile's territory.

With no warning, the adult gator explodes into a charge. Two violent thrashes of its tail send water in every direction as it slams forward, covering 30 feet in seconds. The smaller alligator reacts

Top to bottom: **Juvenile American alligators are typically patterned for their first few years of life. The dark and light bands on this young gator serve to break up its outline. Occasionally, a young gator will be born without skin pigmentation; since it possesses eye pigment, this specimen is actually leucosistic, rather than a true albino.** *Opposite:* **Cloaked in floating duckweed, two American alligators mate in a quiet backwater, the silence broken only by the bull alligator's ritual bellow. Later the bull alligator will have nothing to do with protecting the eggs or young.**

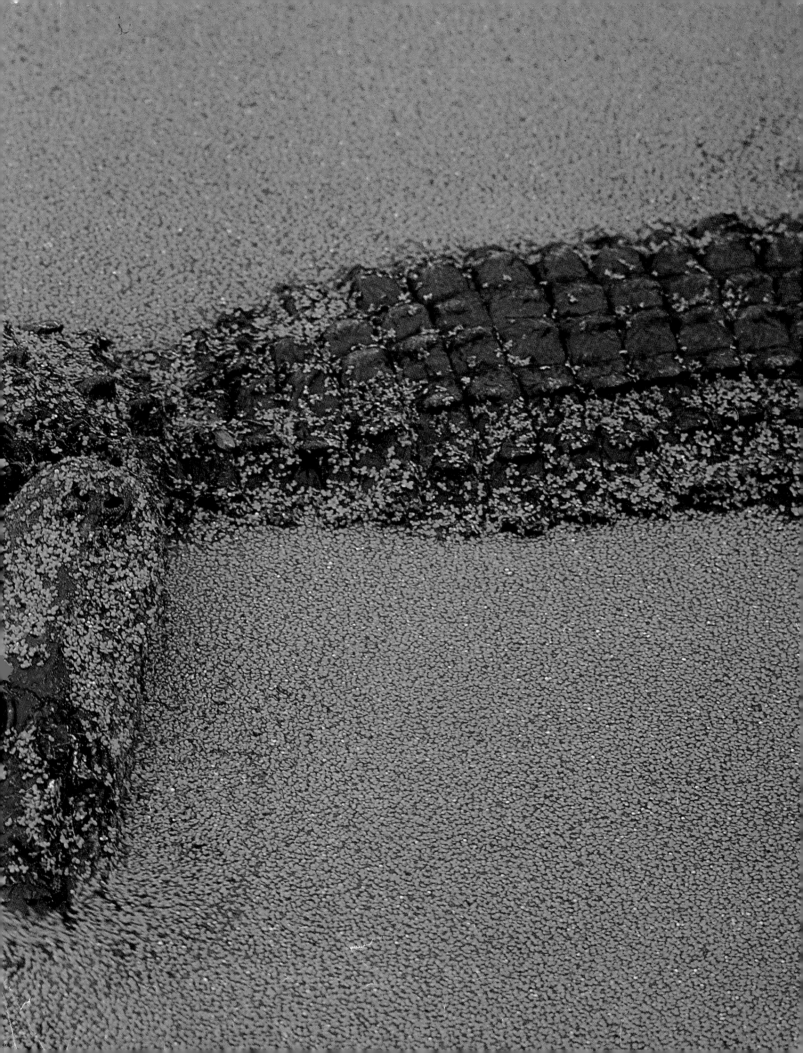

Preceding pages: With their eyes and nostrils positioned high on their heads, all crocodilians can float almost completely submerged, while still breathing and watching for danger. *This page:* American alligators rarely exceed 10 feet in length, although a monster of more than 19 feet was once measured. Like most cold-blooded animals, crocodilians continue to grow for virtually as long as they live—and for some species, that may mean up to 100 years.

Mouth open, an American alligator displays its impressive set of conical teeth, which are designed for grasping rather than cutting. To dismember larger prey, a crocodilian must grab a piece and spin its body; it helps if the prey has been dead a while and is starting to decay.

almost as quickly, twisting toward the cover of the dense fireflags a few yards away. It makes the fireflags with inches to spare, the enraged adult still rocketing headlong in pursuit. Even after the animals are out of sight, the noise of the chase continues, as the wide leaves of the fireflags rock and sway with their passage. A green-backed heron, scared by the ruckus, flaps heavily away from the fight, even as the sounds of splashing taper off.

A few minutes later, the big alligator sails serenely out of the fireflags and back into open water. The interloper is nowhere to be seen – having been taught a lesson, it will steer clear of this particular cove for a while.

There is more to the crocodilians – alligators, crocodiles, and their close relatives – than meets the eye. They are not the evolutionarily backward, dim-witted, slow-moving creatures they might at first seem. They are of ancient lineage, to be sure, but the fact that they have survived for so long in a relatively unchanged form only proves the enduring value of that form, which remains perfectly suited to crocodilians' needs. Moreover, they are more advanced than many reptiles in terms of social interaction and parental care. All in all, they are a fascinating group.

There has always been confusion in distinguishing between alligators, *Family Alligatoridae*, and crocodiles, *Family Crocodylidae*, which only gets further muddied with the addition of caimans (which are in the alligator family), the gavial, *Family Gavialidae*, and some of their close cousins. Collectively, these creatures are known as crocodilians and despite superficial differences of shape and lifestyle, they all share several fundamental traits.

A massive American alligator suns itself on a dry bank. Like all reptiles, crocs have no internal control over their body temperature, and must move from sun to shade to adjust their thermal level.

The "baby alligators" of the pet trade, young caimans are really crocodilians native to Central America and northern South America, where they inhabit freshwater rivers, swamps, and marshes.

Concentrated by the dry season in a
steadily shrinking pool of water, dozens of
turtles crowd around a common caiman,
Caiman crocodilius, in Venezuela—even
using the big reptile as a basking log. The
shared quarters are risky for the turtles,
which might be eaten by the caiman.

Preceding page: **A mature Yacare caiman,** *Caiman crocodilius yacare,* **a subspecies of the common caiman, basks along a Brazilian river next to a heavily traveled haul-out path, the mud deeply scored with the claw marks of caimans.** *This page:* **In the Pantanal, the vast Brazilian swamp created each year by the flooding Paraguay River, Yacare caimans line the banks of the rivers and streams. A threatened animal in most of central South America, the Yacare caiman has been hunted to near extinction in many areas.**

Crocodilians look like big lizards – but looks can be deceiving; they belong to a separate order, *Crocodylia*, which arose nearly 25 million years after lizards first evolved. Crocs (and the term is used here for all members of the clan) are large; adults reach from lengths of six feet to more than 20. They have long muscular tails, heavily plated backs, and elongated snouts, although, generally speaking, crocodiles have longer, thinner snouts than alligators and caimans. All are semi-aquatic, spending their lives in shallow water near shore; their eyes and nostrils are set high on the head and snout, so that the animal can see and breathe with most of its body submerged. All crocs have toothy jaws, and the teeth are set in sockets, rather than fused to the jaw as in lizards and snakes. In the crocodile, the large fourth tooth on the lower jaw is visible when the mouth is closed; however, in the alligator this tooth is concealed. The dentition of crocs closely resembles that of the long extinct dinosaurs – in fact crocs are related to the ancestors of the dinosaurs that arose a few million years after the crocodilians appeared.

Another important difference between crocodilians and lizards can be seen in the way in which each carries itself on land. The hip

Top to bottom: **The broad-snouted caiman,** *Caiman latirostris,* **is found in southern South America, from Brazil through Argentina, Paraguay, and Uruguay. The black caiman,** *Melanosuchus niger,* **largest of the caiman group, is feared in the Amazon basin – accused on scanty evidence of man-eating. The black caiman and other caimans were once so plentiful that they impeded shipping on the river and its tributaries; today their numbers have been greatly reduced by commercial hunting.** *Opposite:* **Only the head of a black caiman protrudes above the silty, weed-choked waters of an oxbow lake in Peru.**

Living evidence of continental drift, the American alligator and Chinese alligator, *Alligator sinensis,* pictured, are the only two survivors of their genus, now separated by thousands of miles of ocean. The Chinese species is found only in the Yangtze River.

The gavial, *Gavialis gangeticus,* of India, Burma, and neighboring countries, is one of the most specialized of the crocodilians, with its extremely narrow snout designed for catching fish, and teeth adapted for holding them.

Another generation of hope for a critically endangered species, young American crocodiles, *Crocodylus acutus,* rest piggyback on a log in the Florida Everglades. Restricted to a few brackish swamps in south Florida, this species is in serious peril.

From the front, the snaggle-toothed jaws of an American crocodile may look the same as an alligator's, but when the jaws are closed, the crocodile's narrow snout is easy to differentiate from the gator's much broader head.

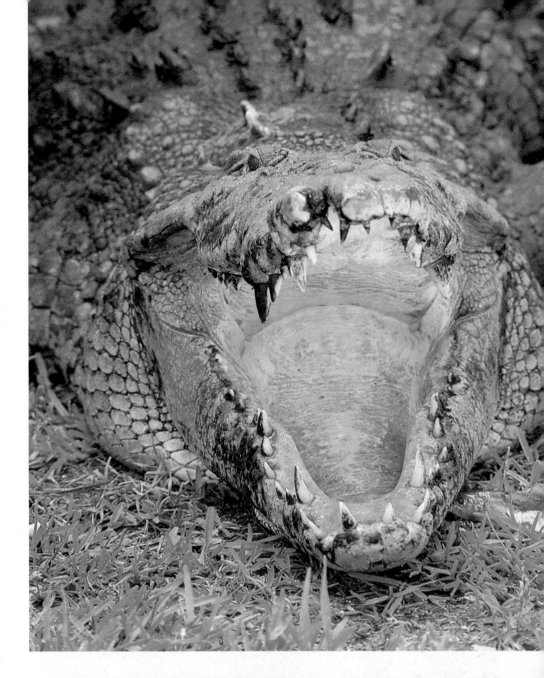

of the lizard lacks a deep socket for the leg bone, and the leg itself is set high on the side of the body, with the femur, or humerus, jutting out almost horizontally; consequently, the lizard moves with its belly dragging the ground, in a spraddle-legged posture. Crocs, on the other hand, have a deeper hip socket and a more erect carriage, with the upper leg bones coming down from the body at a steeper angle. When a crocodilian rouses itself from a snooze by the water, it raises its body well off the ground and keeps its legs closer to its center of gravity. This makes for far more efficient walking – or running, since crocs are capable of attaining remarkable speeds out of the water. One species clocked in at nearly 11 miles an hour, and there have been claims of speeds of more than 20 miles an hour for others.

Once in the water, the croc's tail takes over. Deeply compressed vertically, the tail acts as a scull, propelling the crocodile or alligator through the water. The tail has powerful muscles, and the backbone segments have long prongs rising vertically for support, with smaller horizontal prongs for additional anchoring. Top speed in the water is also around 20 miles an hour for the largest species.

One major difference between crocodilians and other reptiles that is not immediately apparent is the anatomy of the heart. In most reptiles, the heart's lower chambers – the ventricles – are joined near their tops, allowing a partial mixing of oxygen-rich blood, fresh from the lungs, with oxygen-poor blood that

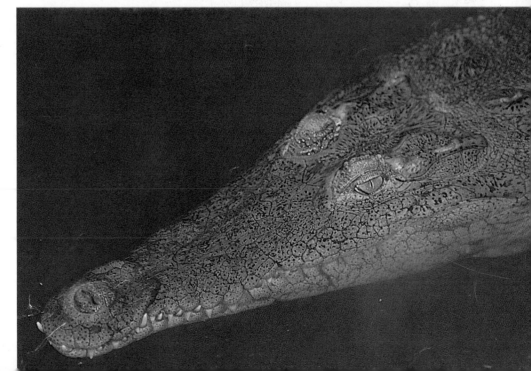

Tucked under a washed-out bank, a large American crocodile is only a few feet from true safety—the water. American crocs are usually less than 12 feet in length, although South American subspecies may exceed 20 feet. While alligators stay in freshwater, crocodiles are partial to salt or brackish water. *Below:* Knobbed and armor-plated, a croc's skin stands up to bites and scratches, both from its prey and from rival crocs. The horny protrusions are called scutes, and provide further protection.

The Cuban crocodile, *Crocodylus rhombifer*, restricted to the island of Cuba, is now found only in two swamps there. It is much more colorful than its relative across the Straits of Florida, the American crocodile.

Hide-hunting in years past has brought the Cuban crocodile to its current endangered position. Relentless destruction for gain or from ignorance has threatened virtually every species of crocodilian in the world; their habit of basking on river banks makes them especially vulnerable.

has already circulated to the body tissues. While this feature is an improvement over the amphibian's heart, which has only a single ventricle, it is far from efficient. Crocodilians, on the other hand, have a primitive version of the four-chambered heart, which is the hallmark of birds and mammals. With this complete separation of the ventricles, and thus the blood flow, the crocs enjoy a more effective circulatory system.

Worldwide, there are 22 species of crocs, found in the warmer latitudes of both hemispheres. Crocodiles are most common in the Old World and Pacific Rim, while alligators and caimans are restricted to the New World, with the exception of the Chinese alligator.

In the United States there are but two species of crocodilians – the American alligator, *Alligator mississippiensis*, and the American crocodile, *Crocodylus acutus*. The alligator is by far the more common of the two, found from the Gulf Coast north to the Carolinas and inland on the coastal plain. Most gators are under 10 feet in length. A six- or seven-foot alligator is considered big in many areas, although the record size for a gator is 19 feet, two inches. The American crocodile averages between seven and 12 feet in length, and is endangered in its limited U.S. range of extreme southern Florida and the Florida Keys. American crocodiles are usually found in brackish or salt water, while alligators prefer fresh-water marshes, swamps, and rivers.

One of the least-known crocs in the world, the Orinoco crocodile, *Crocodylus intermedius*, is found in the Orinoco basin of Columbia and Venezuela. One of the largest crocodilians, it reaches lengths of 23 feet. It is also extremely rare; the International Union for Conservation of Nature has listed it among the 12 most endangered animals in the world.

Preceding page: Inhabitants of eastern Central America, the population of Morelet's crocodiles, *Crocodylus moreletii,* has declined due to hunting pressure and the loss of gallery forests along lowland rivers. *This page:* A Morelet's crocodile lifts its head from the water to survey its surroundings. Although it reaches impressive lengths and inhabits rivers along which humans often live, bathe, and fish, Morelet's crocodile is not usually considered dangerous, and is not feared nearly as much as the caiman.

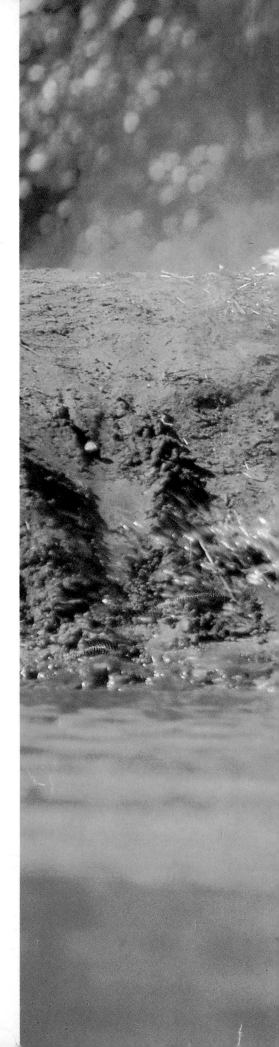

Hitting the water with a splash, a Nile crocodile heads for cover. Although crocs spend a great deal of time basking on land, they are most comfortable in water, and will dive at the first sign of trouble. *Below:* A Nile crocodile, *Crocodylus niloticus,* floats motionlessly among the reeds of a spring in Kenya, waiting for a herd of grazing animals to come to the water for a drink.

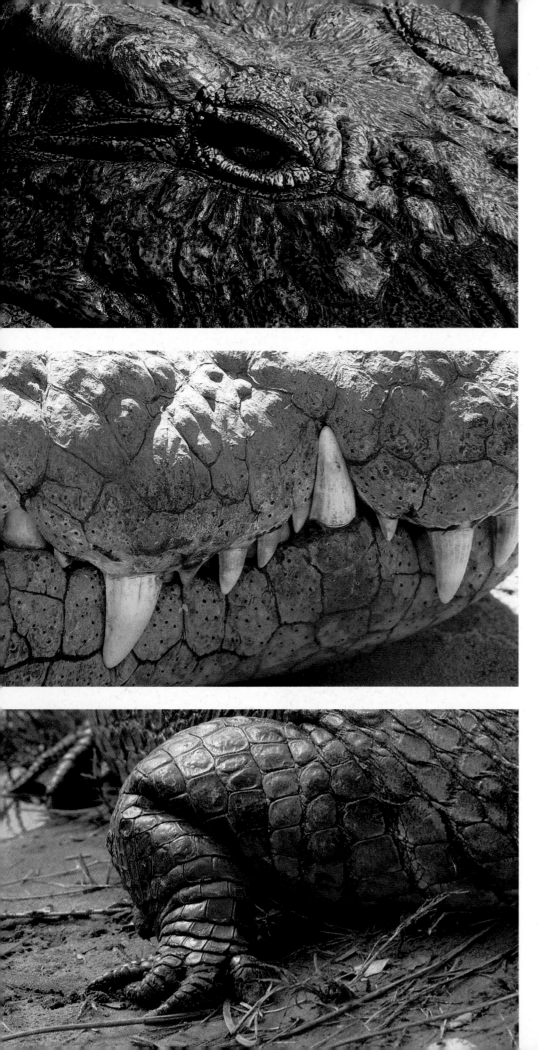

The largest of the crocodilians is the saltwater crocodile of Australia and southeast Asia, *Crocodylus porosus*, which routinely exceeds 20 feet; one monster of 28 feet is on record. That pales in comparison to a prehistoric croc, *Deinosuchus*, which apparently grew to lengths of more than 50 feet. At the other end of the scale are two living species, the common spectacled caiman, *Caiman sclerops*, and West African dwarf crocodile, *Osteolaemus tetraspis*, each with a maximum length of just six feet.

The oddest croc is the gavial (also called gharial) of Asia, *Gavialis gangeticus*, the only species in its family, which has the narrow head of the crocodile, but tapered to the extreme, resulting in a snout that looks like a pencil with a bulbous eraser (prominent in males) at the end. Inhabiting rivers, the gavial feeds on fish, which it captures by lashing its open mouth from side to side; because the snout is so thin and streamlined, the gavial can make lightning-fast grabs even underwater.

Most crocs are fish-eaters to some degree, although they are opportunists that will rarely pass up any potential food item of the right size. Turtles, aquatic mammals, birds, and snakes are regularly taken, and larger crocodilians, like the Nile croc of Africa, *Crocodylus niloticus*, will hunt antelope and other relatively large mammals; the

Top to bottom: **The well-made croc: A Nile crocodile shows the physical adaptations that aid it and its semi-aquatic life-style. Just behind the eye, a flap all but closes the croc's ear opening; the rows of teeth jut from the jaws even when the mouth is closed. The feet are not webbed and are not used for swimming (the tail is), but are strong enough for short bursts of speed on land.**

Water moistens the hide of a Nile crocodile, bringing out an unexpectedly beautiful pattern of brown and yellow in the head scales. *Overleaf:* Looking more sluggish than it really is, a massive Nile croc lumbers across a sandbar. Its nearly erect walk—common to all crocodilians—allows it to move quickly if necessary.

The aptly named slender-snouted crocodile, *Crocodylus cataphractus*, is found in freshwater rivers and swamps in central and western Africa. Only in the Congo is the species even relatively secure; elsewhere its population has declined significantly.

Looking more like an alligator, the African dwarf crocodile, *Osteolaemus tetraspis,* rarely grows longer than six feet. Native to tropical rivers in west Africa, it is among the rarest of the world's crocodilians.

saltwater croc often takes water buffalo. Crocs are masters at the art of ambush, slipping unnoticed toward their intended victims, then using their immensely strong tails to close the gap with a stunning lunge. The jaws clamp shut with incredible power, gripping hard as the croc dives; most vertebrate prey is killed by a combination of massive wounds and drowning as the croc rolls with it underwater.

Unable to chew, crocs eat by grabbing a mouthful and rolling or thrashing, tearing the meat free. Smaller prey is simply chomped into bite-sized pieces and swallowed. Eating, as with most activities in a croc's life, takes place in the water, but at the surface rather than below. If there is more food than a crocodilian can eat in one sitting – or if it is not immediately hungry – it may cache its kill by jamming it among sunken tree branches, or beneath an undercut riverbank.

While on the subject of food, a word must be said about man-eaters. About a third of the crocodilian species around the world have been known to attack humans, most often from a sense of territoriality than hunger. The worst offender may be the Nile crocodile; in some parts of Africa, the toll has been estimated at 30 or 40 people a month along croc-rich lakes. The saltwater croc is another proven man-eater. While that's not surprising considering its great size, it

Crocs look like holdovers from the Age of Dinosaurs, and while they are certainly ancient, they are neither descendants of the dinosaurs nor "living fossils." Crocodilians have a relatively advanced heart structure, but they lack the ability to regulate their body temperature, which some scientists now believe the dinosaurs were able to do.

Preceding page: Buck-toothed fangs jut from the snout of a false gavial, *Tomistoma schlegelii*, of Malaysia and parts of Indonesia. Although it is not closely related to the true gavial, the false gavial shares its fish-eating habits, hence the elongated snout for quick movement under-water. *This page:* The false gavial is so distinct from other crocodilians that scientists have sometimes placed it in its own family; others argue that it belongs with the true crocodiles, but separate from the alligators and caimans, and from the true gavial.

Preceding pages: Black as the water in which it floats, a mugger crocodile, *Crocodylus palustris,* patrols silently for prey. The mugger is the dominant croc over much of the Indian subcontinent, where it is reputed to be a man-eater. Many experts, however, believe it most often scavenges the remains of incomplete cremations, and only rarely attacks living humans. *This page, left:* The mugger crocodile does not reach the great lengths of some of its relatives, with a maximum of 13 to 15 feet. *Below:* While most crocs would welcome a meal of a wading bird, egrets like this one in Sri Lanka have little to worry about, as long as they do not wander too close to a hidden crocodile.

Stretched out on the sandbar of an Indian river, mugger crocodiles soak in the sun. Protection and captive breeding have benefited mugger crocs in India, a country that is better known for its work with gavials.

actually kills far less often than claimed. One well-circulated story purports that "salties" ate most of a 1,000-man Japanese garrison retreating through the swamps of Ramree Island in the Bay of Bengal, during the waning days of World War II. In truth, while a few men may have died from croc attacks, the vast majority of the garrison made it through safely. Even in Australia, where saltwater crocodiles were once extraordinarily common (and where, despite a century of exploitation, they are still found in many northern rivers and swamps), only about 20 deaths in more than 100 years can be blamed on the species – and many of those were croc hunters who gave their quarry more than enough provocation for attack.

The American alligator, whose numbers are increasing and which is now found in many suburban locations in the South, is not dangerous under most circumstances, but people who foolishly feed gators may create deadly problems. Several people and many pets have been killed in alligator encounters since the early 1970's. Alligators should always be treated with respect and caution.

Stray shafts of light, penetrating the rain forest canopy, illuminate a Siamese crocodile, *Crocodylus siamensis*. The broad, plated tails of all crocs are designed for swimming, with special vertical and horizontal prongs jutting from the backbone to anchor powerful muscles.
***Following page:* Basking crocodilians, like this Siamese croc, often orient their open mouths to the sun, allowing its heat to warm the blood-rich linings of the jaws. A special flap, known as the false palate, closes off the throat when the animal opens its mouth underwater; it must surface to eat.**

Crocodilians of all kinds tend to be most aggressive during the breeding season, when males bellow to attract females, and display with tail splashes and a peculiar vibration of the sides that makes the water around them shiver and dance. At night, the roar of a bull alligator reverberates through the swamps for amazing distances.

Once mated, the female looks for a place to lay her eggs. For some species, like the Nile crocodile, that means a sandy bank out of reach of flood waters, often the same spot year after year, where she will dig a hole, deposit several dozen leathery eggs, and spend little or no time at the nest. Likewise, female American crocodiles dig a hole in the sand, lay their eggs, and forget them until the hatchlings emerge. American alligators, on the other hand, build mounds of rotting vegetation that may be seven feet across, and which are carefully tended to keep the internal temperature at an optimum level. The nesting season may last from spring until late summer or early autumn, and the female gator generally stays nearby most of the time, not hesitating to attack intruders, including humans.

The young, like those of all reptiles, are self-sufficient from the moment they emerge from the shells of their eggs. But unlike most other reptiles, which abandon their young at egg-laying or birth, crocodilian mothers are attentive parents

Preceding page: **The ridged skin of a Siamese crocodile hardly seems like the stuff of fashion, but the smooth leather of its soft belly has long been a favorite of humans, and has led to the destruction of millions of crocs worldwide and the decimation of almost of every species.** *These pages:* **Also known as the freshwater croc,** *Crocodylus johnstonii* **inhabits rivers and swamps in Australia.**

Preceding page: Flickering sun on dark water paints an abstract picture, with an Australian freshwater crocodile as the subject. *This page:* The tapered jaws of the freshwater crocodile, armed with especially long teeth, are designed for hunting fish. Like all crocs, this species frequently loses its teeth during attacks and while eating; spares quickly grow to replace the missing fangs.

Preceding page: One of the most imposing animals in the world, the saltwater crocodile, *Crocodylus porosus,* also known as the estuarine croc, surpasses lengths of 23 feet, and there are old, unsubstantiated records of males of more than 30 feet. This 20-foot-long male is eating a handout — a chicken. *This page, top to bottom:* Along a muddy estuary creek at low tide, a "saltie" rests in the open. Crocodilians will spend the better part of the day basking in the sun, becoming active in the early evening. When hunting, all crocodiles rely on a submerged (or almost submerged) approach and a sudden, terrifying lunge, grabbing their prey and pulling back into the water to drown it.

for at least a few weeks (and sometimes as long as two years). The young do not have to be fed, as do baby birds or mammals, but the adult provides protection against herons, raccoons, and other dangers that the nine-inch hatchlings might face. Some crocs take the process a step further: Colonial nesting and sharing of guard duties has been observed, and croc mothers, alerted by the squeaks of their hatching babies, may excavate the nest hole and help them out of their eggs, using jaws that can kill a zebra to gingerly break the shells and carry the infants to safety.

With all their adaptations, one might expect life to be easy for a crocodilian, but in fact, virtually all of the world's species are in various states of danger: 20 species and subspecies are listed as endangered or threatened. The very hide that protects them from attack makes them vulnerable to humans, since crocodile leather is prized by the fashion world. In addition, some species (like the American alligator) are popular as food, and many are shot simply because they are considered a dangerous nuisance. By some estimates, 20 million crocodilians were killed in the past 50 years, primarily for their hides.

Saltwater crocodiles inhabit an extremely wide range of areas. Although best-known as inhabitants of Australia, they are also found from India to the New Hebrides, and were once native as far north as south China. Because it often crosses open water (in one case more than 800 miles of ocean), this species has colonized most of the islands of Indonesia.

While there is no doubt that saltwater crocodiles are dangerous, causing about 20 human deaths in the past century in Australia, they are not the constant menace they are sometimes portrayed to be.

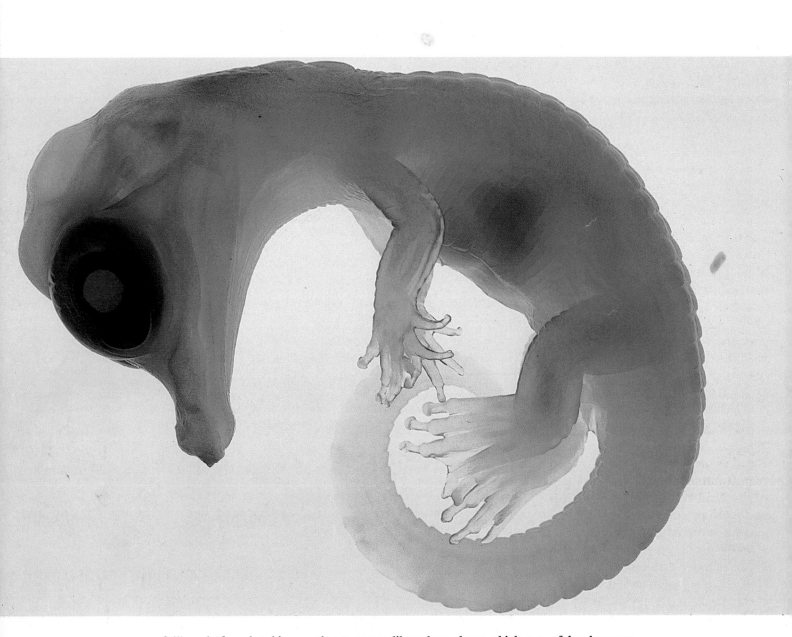

Still weeks from hatching, a saltwater crocodile embryo shows a high state of development. By carefully regulating the amount of rotting vegetation on the nest mound, a female croc can maintain the proper temperature for her eggs.

Habitat loss, such as the loss of suitable river locations for the gavial, is an even greater danger in many areas.

The conflict between humans and crocs is exemplified by the saltwater crocodile. All but wiped out in many parts of its southeast Asian range, the saltie also suffered serious losses in Australia's Northern Territory during the past century, as professional croc hunters killed untold numbers for the hide trade. The saltwater croc population, once numbering perhaps a million, had dropped to a fraction of its original level by 1970, at which time legal protection was belatedly granted. Today, saltwater crocs appear to be increasing, although the rate of increase and total population size are hotly contested. Clearly though, in many areas, burgeoning numbers of people are coming in direct conflict with the crocs, which have attacked boats and killed livestock – as well as an occasional human.

The recovery of the American alligator has also been a double-edged sword. In 1973, the gator, its population thought to have been decimated by poaching, was placed under the protection of the Endangered Species Act. While there may actually have been more alligators in the swamps than biologists realized, the gator's own fecundity played a role in its rebound, and today there are millions across the

Top to bottom: **Young salties poke out from their eggs in a nest mound that has been opened by researchers; ordinarily, the mother would aggressively chase any intruders away from the nest and help the young emerge herself. For several months thereafter, she stays with her hatchlings to protect them – one of the greatest displays of maternal care among reptiles.**

South. Increasingly, gators are living not in remote bayous, but in golf course water hazards, park canals, and even, on occasion, in backyard swimming pools. To control the rapidly swelling gator population, legal hunting seasons have been instituted, with both hides and meat finding a ready market. Rigorously controlled to avoid the sort of slaughter that landed the gators in trouble once before, hunting seasons pump billions of dollars into local economies, and provide a powerful incentive to preserve wetlands.

In other parts of the world, crocs are getting a helping hand from humans. Commercial "croc farming" has taken some of the pressure off wild populations, and some species, like the gavial, have benefited from refuge and reintroduction programs. It may be that the tide of public opinion has finally turned in favor of these massive, armor-clad beasts that embody a visible link to the earth's distant, reptilian past.

Incoming waves swallow an average-sized saltwater crocodile. Despite their name, salties generally avoid the surf, and are most often found in quiet tidal areas; they may also travel far upriver from the ocean.

A blooming water lily provides a counterpoint for the primitive shape of a saltwater crocodile, basking on the shore of an overgrown lagoon. *Overleaf:* Sunset tints a saltwater croc at rest in Queensland, Australia. With protection, saltwater crocodiles are recovering from years of unrestricted killing in many parts of Australia.

Index of Photography

TIB indicates The Image Bank

DEP.LEG. B-15.692-91